TOPMARQUES

LUXURY CARS

ROB COLSON

WAYLAND

First published in 2015 by Wayland
Copyright © Wayland 2015

Wayland
338 Euston Road
London NW1 3BH

Wayland Australia
Level 17/207 Kent Street
Sydney, NSW 2000

Editor: Elizabeth Brent

Produced for Wayland by
Tall Tree Ltd
Designed by Jonathan Vipond

ISBN 978 0 7502 8590 2

eBook ISBN 978 0 7502 9465 2

Dewey number: 629.2'222-dc23

10 9 8 7 6 5 4 3 2 1

Printed in China

Wayland is a division of
Hachette Children's Books,
an Hachette UK company
www.hachette.co.uk

Please note: the website addresses (URLs) included in this book were valid at the time of going to press. However, because of the nature of the Internet, it is possible that some addresses may have changed, or sites may have changed or closed down since publication. While the author and publishers regret any inconvenience this may cause to the readers, no responsibility for any such changes can be accepted by either the author or the publishers.

⚙ KEY TO ABBREVIATIONS

MM = millimetre

KM/H = kilometres per hour

HP = horsepower

RPM = revs per minute

CC = cubic centimetre

L/100KM = litres per 100 kilometres

G/KM = grams per kilometre

Words in **bold** appear in the glossary.

The publisher would like to thank the following for their kind permission to reproduce their photographs:

Key: (t) top; (c) centre; (b) bottom; (l) left; (r) right

Front Cover: Steve Lagreca/Dreamstime.com, Back Cover t: Philip Lange/Shutterstock.com, Back Cover b: Steve Lagreca/Dreamstime.com, 1 Rolls-Royce Motor Cars, 2 GuoZhongHua/Shutterstock.com, 3 Bentley Motors, 4–5 Mercedes-Benz, 5t Art Konovalov/Shutterstock.com, 5b Mercedes-Benz, 6–7 Beltane43/Creative Commons Sharealike, 6b Bocman1973/Shutterstock.com, 7t VanderWolf Images/Shutterstock.com, 7c Edvvc/Creative Ccommons Attribution, 7b Bocman1973/Shutterstock.com, 8–9, 9t Rolls-Royce Motor Cars 9b Teddy Leung/Shutterstock.com, 10, 11t, 11c, 11b Audi AG, 12–13, 13t, 13b BMW Group, 14–15, 15t, 15b Toyota PLC, 16–17, 17t, 17b Porsche Cars, 18–19, 19t, 19b Bentley Motors, 20-21, 21t, 21b Infiniti, 22–23, 23t, 23b Jaguar Land Rover Ltd, 24, 24–25, 25 Cadillac Photos, 26b, 26–27, 27b Mercedes-Benz, 28–29 1000 Words/Shutterstock.com, 29t D. Winslow/Creative Commons Sharealike, 29b Pete Souza, 30 Toyota PLC, 31 Audi AG

CONTENTS

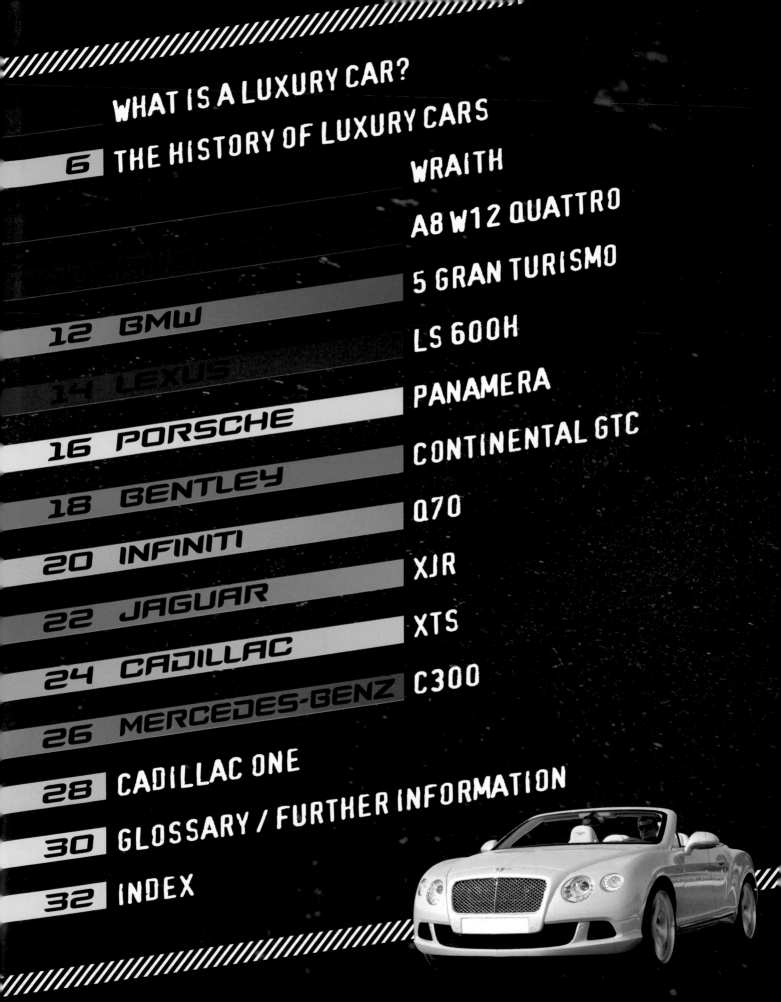

WHAT IS A LUXURY CAR?

TV SCREENS
Passengers in the back seats have their own 250mm screens to watch movies.

SUSPENSION
Suspension rods are attached to the wheels. The rods have springs attached. They give a smoother ride and better handling around corners.

SEATS
Soft leather seats are fully adjustable and individually heated.

A luxury car is a vehicle designed to allow its driver and passengers to travel in maximum comfort. Made using the finest materials and the latest technology, luxury cars are exciting to drive and a pleasure to ride.

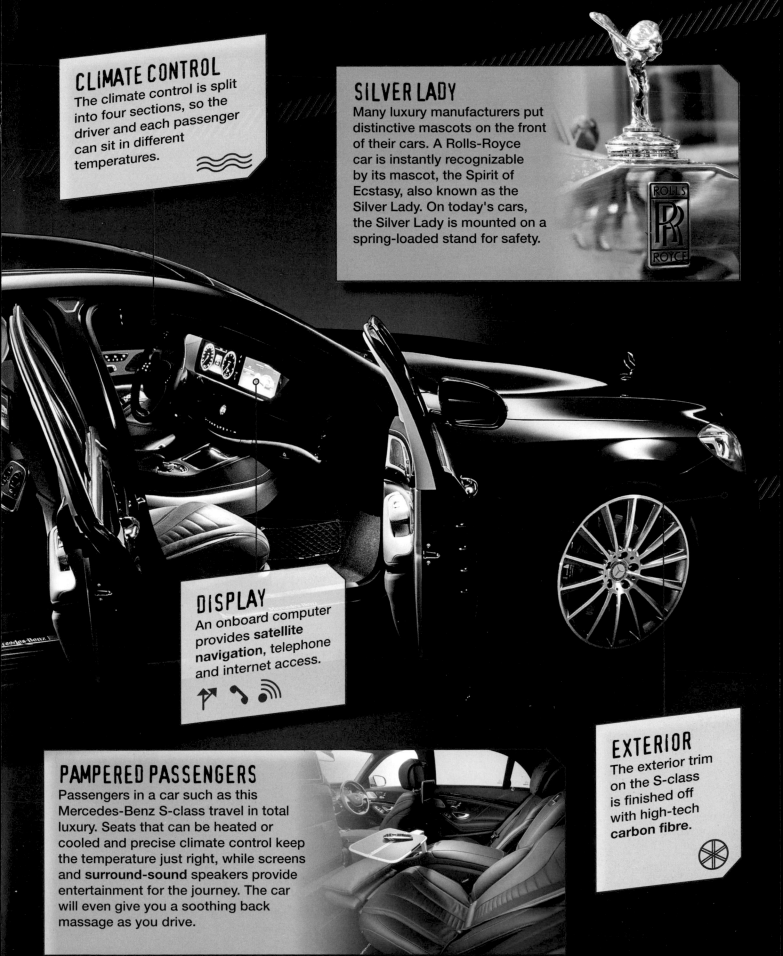

CLIMATE CONTROL
The climate control is split into four sections, so the driver and each passenger can sit in different temperatures.

SILVER LADY
Many luxury manufacturers put distinctive mascots on the front of their cars. A Rolls-Royce car is instantly recognizable by its mascot, the Spirit of Ecstasy, also known as the Silver Lady. On today's cars, the Silver Lady is mounted on a spring-loaded stand for safety.

DISPLAY
An onboard computer provides **satellite navigation**, telephone and internet access.

EXTERIOR
The exterior trim on the S-class is finished off with high-tech **carbon fibre**.

PAMPERED PASSENGERS
Passengers in a car such as this Mercedes-Benz S-class travel in total luxury. Seats that can be heated or cooled and precise climate control keep the temperature just right, while screens and **surround-sound** speakers provide entertainment for the journey. The car will even give you a soothing back massage as you drive.

THE HISTORY OF LUXURY CARS

In the early days of motoring, before World War Two, powerful cars were the preserve of the rich and famous. From the 1950s, new technology allowed many more people to afford a touch of luxury. Manufacturers such as Citroën, BMW and Mercedes-Benz targeted new markets by offering luxury options on many of their cars.

1927–1933

BUGATTI

ROYALE

The Bugatti Type 41, better known as the Royale, is one of the largest cars ever built. Its 610-mm wheels were powered by an enormous 12.7-litre engine. Designed to be the most luxurious car ever made, it was intended for European royalty. However, it proved too expensive, and only six cars were ever built.

TOP SPEED:
160 KM/H

1955–1975

CITROËN

DS

The Citroën DS was fitted with a revolutionary new **hydraulic** suspension system. Instead of springs, the suspension was connected to a sphere containing pressurized nitrogen. This automatically corrected the suspension to ensure that a constant height was maintained, giving the car an ultra-smooth ride.

TOP SPEED:
165 KM/H

AMERICAN GLAMOUR

During the 1950s, large numbers of people in the USA began to earn enough money to afford luxury cars. Big family cars such as the 1958 Buick Super (pictured here) became best-sellers. The Super had a 6-litre V8 engine.

1959–1968

ROLLS-ROYCE

TOP SPEED:
163 KM/H

PHANTOM V

The choice of kings and presidents, the Phantom V was a status symbol in the 1960s, showing the wealth and power of the owner. In 1965, pop star John Lennon bought this Phantom V and had it painted in colourful patterns.

1972–1980

MERCEDES-BENZ

W116

During the 1970s, the German car manufacturer Mercedes-Benz started to give their customers lists of optional luxury extras. The W116 was their flagship model. Luxury options included wipers on the headlights, and air conditioning controlled by the latest electronics systems.

TOP SPEED:
225 KM/H

ROLLS-ROYCE
WRAITH

Named after a model that was first made in 1938, the two-doored Wraith is Rolls-Royce's sportiest car. It combines high **performance** with the comfort of a luxury car. Even at high speeds, the computer-controlled 'air' suspension ensures a super-smooth ride.

The windscreen slopes backwards to make the car aerodynamic.

The car has the distinctive rectangular radiator grille typical of Rolls-Royce designs.

FRONT WHEELS:
510 x 215 MM

TOP SPEED: **250** KM/H | 0–100 KM/H: **4.6** SECONDS

ENGINE:
6600 CC

CYLINDERS:
V12

GEARBOX:
8-SPEED

TRANSMISSION:
REAR-WHEEL DRIVE

Hand-woven into the lining of the roof are 1,340 tiny **fibre-optic** lights. At night, the lights give the impression that you are driving under a clear, starry sky. They can be adjusted to give a faint, relaxing glow or shine brightly enough to read by.

The large coach-style doors are hinged at the rear.

REAR WHEELS:
510 x 240 MM

COMPUTERIZED GEARBOX

The 12-cylinder engine is connected to the wheels by an 8-speed **gearbox**. The gearbox is linked to a satellite navigation system. A computer is fed information about the road ahead, such as corners or hills, and the car changes gear automatically before the driver is even aware that the corner or hill is there.

The large engine and computer-controlled **transmission** make the Wraith the most powerful Rolls-Royce ever.

MAXIMUM POWER: 624 HP AT 5600 RPM

SUSPENSION:	BODY:	BRAKES:	FUEL CONSUMPTION:	CO₂ EMISSION:
DOUBLE WISHBONE	ALUMINIUM	CERAMIC DISCS	14 L/100 KM	327 G/KM

BMW
5 GRAN TURISMO

The Gran Turismo is a spacious car designed for driving long distances in style. BMW make a range of models. The Luxury model has the largest engine and best performance. It has a hatchback boot to store all the luggage needed for a long journey.

FRONT WHEELS:
480 x 215 MM

TOP SPEED: 250 KM/H | **0-100 KM/H:** 5 SECONDS

ENGINE:	CYLINDERS:	GEARBOX:	TRANSMISSION:
4395 CC	V8	8-SPEED	REAR-WHEEL DRIVE

⚙ CUTTING EDGE

The car has a high roof to provide more space inside. The high driving position gives the driver an excellent view of the road ahead.

A large sun roof floods the interior with natural light. The sun roof slides and lifts to let air in. Wind deflectors ensure that the air does not swirl around unpleasantly inside the car. This also keeps noise down to a minimum.

The panoramic sun roof opens and closes at the touch of a button.

REAR WHEELS:
480x240 MM

The wheels are made of a light alloy. Their distinctive multi-spoke design makes them light but strong.

ACTIVE STEERING
When the car takes corners, both the front and the rear wheels turn. At under 60 km/h, the rear wheels turn in the opposite direction to the front wheels. This gives the car a smaller turning circle. At more than 60 km/h, both wheels turn in the same direction, making the car more stable.

MAXIMUM POWER: 450 HP AT 6000 RPM

SUSPENSION:	BODY:	BRAKES:	FUEL CONSUMPTION:	CO₂ EMISSION:
MULTI-ARM AXLE	ALUMINIUM	ALUMINIUM DISCS	9.2 L/100 KM	214 G/KM

LEXUS LS 600H

REAR WHEELS:
480 x 245 MM

A long wheelbase (the distance between front and rear wheels) makes the car very stable.

The LS600 is a **hybrid,** which means that it is powered by both a petrol engine and an electric motor. At speeds of up to 65 km/h, it glides along almost silently on its electric motor. At higher speeds, the petrol engine takes over. To accelerate, the engine and motor work together to produce extra power.

The underlayers of the paintwork contain aluminium flakes, which sparkle in sunlight.

TOP SPEED: 250 KM/H   0–100 KM/H: 6.3 SECONDS

ENGINE:	CYLINDERS:	GEARBOX:	TRANSMISSION:
4969 CC WITH INTEGRATED ELECTRIC MOTOR	V8	7-SPEED	ALL-WHEEL DRIVE

TOTAL COMFORT

Passengers adjust the seats using controls on the arm rest. They can even give themselves a massage, which is delivered by eight air pockets in the seats.

Control panel

This modified LS 600H sits close to the ground, giving it a sportier look.

FRONT WHEELS:
480 x 245 MM

⚙ CUTTING EDGE

The wing mirrors of cars have 'blind spots'. This means that another car may be close but not appear on the mirror. Radars in the rear bumper detect nearby cars. A warning signal flashes in the mirror if the driver tries to change lane when another car is in the blind spot in the next lane.

MAXIMUM POWER (COMBINED): 445 HP AT 6400 RPM

SUSPENSION:
MULTILINK AIR

BODY:
ALUMINIUM/
STEEL

BRAKES:
VENTILATED
DISCS

FUEL CONSUMPTION:
8.6 L/100 KM

CO₂ EMISSION:
199 G/KM

PORSCHE
PANAMERA

The body is made from a mix of high-strength steel, stainless steel, aluminium and magnesium.

Exhaust pipes

The Panamera is a luxury sports car that can be fitted with a normal petrol engine or a hybrid engine. The body and engine are built using lightweight metals such as aluminium and magnesium to give maximum performance and efficiency.

REAR WHEELS:
460 x 230 MM

TOP SPEED: **270** KM/H | 0–100 KM/H: **5.5** SECONDS

ENGINE:
2995 CC WITH INTEGRATED ELECTRIC MOTOR

CYLINDERS:
6

GEARBOX:
7-SPEED

TRANSMISSION:
REAR-WHEEL DRIVE

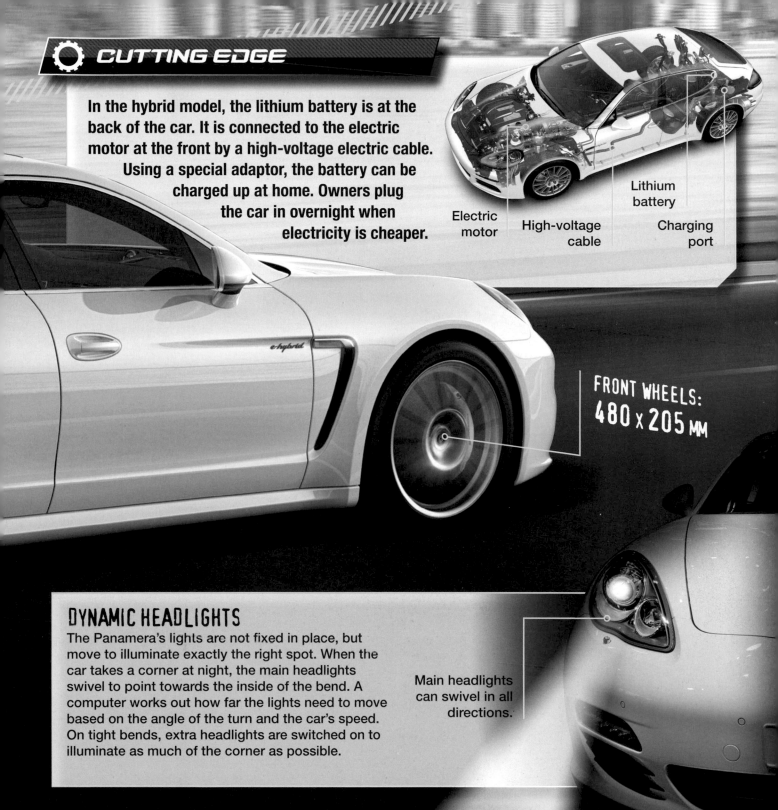

In the hybrid model, the lithium battery is at the back of the car. It is connected to the electric motor at the front by a high-voltage electric cable. Using a special adaptor, the battery can be charged up at home. Owners plug the car in overnight when electricity is cheaper.

Electric motor

High-voltage cable

Lithium battery

Charging port

FRONT WHEELS:
480 x 205 MM

DYNAMIC HEADLIGHTS

The Panamera's lights are not fixed in place, but move to illuminate exactly the right spot. When the car takes a corner at night, the main headlights swivel to point towards the inside of the bend. A computer works out how far the lights need to move based on the angle of the turn and the car's speed. On tight bends, extra headlights are switched on to illuminate as much of the corner as possible.

Main headlights can swivel in all directions.

MAXIMUM POWER: 416 HP AT 5500 RPM

SUSPENSION:
STEEL SPRING

BODY:
STEEL/ALUMINIUM/
MAGNESIUM

BRAKES:
CERAMIC
DISCS

FUEL CONSUMPTION:
3.1 L/100 KM

CO₂ EMISSION:
71 G/KM

BENTLEY
CONTINENTAL GTC

The British manufacturer Bentley has been making luxury cars for nearly 100 years. The Continental GTC is Bentley's latest model. It is a big, powerful car with a soft roof that retracts automatically.

Windscreen frame is reinforced to give it extra strength with the roof down.

FRONT WHEELS:
510 x 275 MM

TOP SPEED: **314** KM/H | 0-100 KM/H: **4.7** SECONDS

ENGINE:	CYLINDERS:	GEARBOX:	TRANSMISSION:
5998 CC	W12	8-SPEED	ALL-WHEEL DRIVE

⚙ CUTTING EDGE

The roof retracts in 25 seconds to give an open-air ride. On a hot summer day, the leather seats are kept cool by a system of fans that draws heat out of the backrests. On colder days, a neck warmer sends out a stream of warm air to take the chill off.

Soft leather

Racing-style bucket seats

Touchscreen computer display

Cool-touch metal fascia

EXTRA GRIP

During winter, the tyres may need to be fitted with snow chains. The chains give the tyres extra grip on snowy or icy roads.

Chain is held loosely around the tyre.

REAR WHEELS: 510 x 275 MM

MAXIMUM POWER: 567 HP AT 6000 RPM

SUSPENSION: AIR SPRINGS

BODY: ALUMINIUM

BRAKES: CARBON-CERAMIC DISCS

FUEL CONSUMPTION: 14.9 L/100 KM

CO₂ EMISSION: 347 G/KM

INFINITI

Q70

The Q70 is designed to make driving easy. Cameras help the driver to see what is around them, while special speakers cancel out the engine's noise and keep the cabin quiet. For efficiency, the accelerator pedal pushes back at the driver's foot if they are wasting fuel.

The aerodynamic shape of the windscreen directs air over the car.

REAR WHEELS:
460 x 245 MM

Scratch-proof paint is elastic, and self-repairs small scratches to the bodywork.

FRONT WHEELS:
460 x 225 MM

TOP SPEED: **250** KM/H | 0-100 KM/H: **6.2** SECONDS

ENGINE:
3696 CC

CYLINDERS:
V6

GEARBOX:
7-SPEED

TRANSMISSION:
REAR-WHEEL DRIVE

Four exhaust pipes remove fumes from the engine.

VARIABLE VALVES

For an engine to work properly, it is crucial that the right amount of air and exhaust gases are allowed in and out. The flow of these gases is controlled by valves, which open and close many times a second. The Q70 is fitted with a variable valve control. It allows more air in at high speeds and less air in at lower speeds. This improves efficiency and reduces harmful emissions.

The bonnet, boot lid and doors are made from lightweight aluminium.

⚙ CUTTING EDGE

The screen next to the driver can show maps, information about the engine, or even a bird's-eye view of the car and its surroundings to help the driver to park. This view is provided by four cameras on the outside of the car.

Screen can show many different kinds of information.

MAXIMUM POWER: 315 HP AT 7000 RPM

SUSPENSION: DOUBLE WISHBONE

BODY: HIGH-STRENGTH STEEL / ALUMINIUM

BRAKES: VENTILATED DISCS

FUEL CONSUMPTION: 10.2 L/100 KM

CO₂ EMISSION: 235 G/KM

JAGUAR

XJR

The XJ has been Jaguar's flagship luxury car since 1968. The latest model, the XJR, packs a powerful punch when overtaking. Press the pedal to the floor, and the supercharged V8 engine will accelerate the car from 80 km/h to 120 km/h in just 2.5 seconds.

Most of the car's body parts are made from lightweight aluminium.

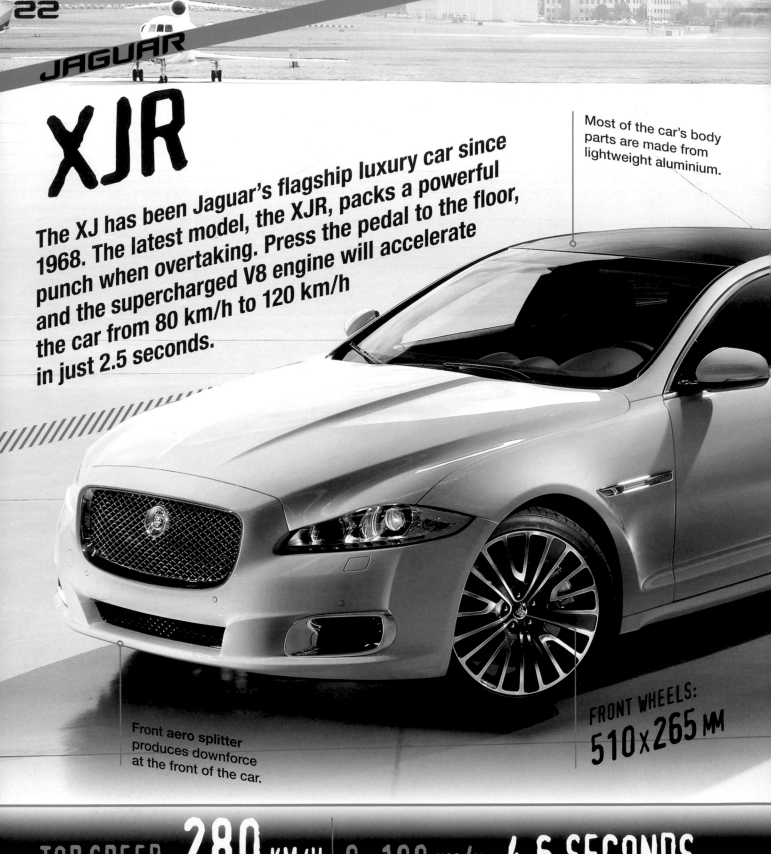

Front aero splitter produces downforce at the front of the car.

FRONT WHEELS:
510 x 265 MM

TOP SPEED: **280** KM/H | 0–100 KM/H: **4.6 SECONDS**

ENGINE:
5000 CC

CYLINDERS:
V8

GEARBOX:
8-SPEED

TRANSMISSION:
REAR-WHEEL DRIVE

CUTTING EDGE

Although it performs like a sports car, the XJR is fully equipped with luxury fittings to ensure a smooth ride. The noise from its huge engine is cancelled out using special speakers, and at lower speeds, passengers glide along in near silence.

Soft leather seats

Control panels in the centre and on the roof

Surround-sound speaker system

Each passenger has their own screen

REAR WHEELS: 510 x 295 MM

Lip spoiler on the boot lid creates downforce.

FAST CORNERING

The XJR can take corners at high speeds. A **spoiler** on the boot disrupts the air flow to produce downforce, helping the car to grip the road on corners. The automatic transmission senses how tight the corner is and keeps the car in the correct gear just long enough to negotiate it safely.

MAXIMUM POWER: 540 HP AT 6500 RPM

SUSPENSION: AIR SUSPENSION

BODY: ALUMINIUM

BRAKES: VENTILATED DISCS

FUEL CONSUMPTION: 11.6 L/100 KM

CO$_2$ EMISSION: 270 G/KM

CADILLAC
XTS

The XTS is a spacious saloon car. It has front-wheel drive, which means that the engine powers the front wheels. Without the need to transfer power from the engine at the front to the wheels at the back, there is more room inside the cabin and the car is more economical to run.

Sculpted wing mirrors allow air to slip over them, reducing noise.

Some of the controls are operated using voice recognition technology.

DISPLAYS AND CONTROLS

The digital display in front of the steering wheel tells the driver everything they need to know without taking their eyes away from the road, including speed, revs and even the tyre pressure. Many controls are positioned on the steering wheel, within easy reach of the thumbs.

FRONT WHEELS:
510 x 245 MM

TOP SPEED: **220** KM/H | 0–100 KM/H: **6.7** SECONDS

ENGINE:	CYLINDERS:		GEARBOX:		TRANSMISSION:
3600 CC	V6		6-SPEED		FRONT-WHEEL DRIVE

The magnetic ride control system checks the road conditions 1,000 times every second. It uses the information to adjust the suspension constantly. This ensures that the tyres are gripping the road at all times, giving sure handling around corners.

REAR WHEELS:
510 x 245 MM

Angular rear lights are a Cadillac trademark.

MAXIMUM POWER: 305 HP AT 6800 RPM

SUSPENSION:	BODY:	BRAKES:	FUEL CONSUMPTION:	CO₂ EMISSION:
FRONT: COIL	ALUMINIUM	VENTILATED	10 L/100 KM	275 G/KM
REAR: AIR	AND STEEL	DISCS		

SUSPENSION: FRONT: COIL REAR: AIR — BODY: ALUMINIUM AND STEEL — BRAKES: VENTILATED DISCS — FUEL CONSUMPTION: 10 L/100 KM — CO$_2$ EMISSION: 275 G/KM

MERCEDES-BENZ

C300

The Mercedes-Benz C300 is a compact four-door saloon designed for maximum safety and efficiency. It is a hybrid car with a diesel engine and an electric motor, which makes it very economical to run.

Smooth lines on the sides of the car give it an aerodynamic shape.

FRONT AND
REAR WHEELS:
480 x 245 MM

CUTTING EDGE

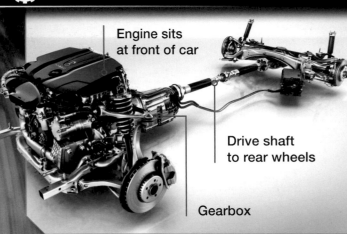

Engine sits
at front of car

Drive shaft
to rear wheels

Gearbox

The power of the engine is carried to the wheels along a **powertrain**. Power passes through the gearbox and along a **driveshaft** that runs underneath the car to the rear wheels. The process is controlled by a computer system, which ensures a minimum of energy loss. **Exhaust** fumes are reused by a **turbocharger** to make the car even more efficient.

TOP SPEED: **245** KM/H | 0-100 KM/H: **6.4** SECONDS

ENGINE:
2143 CC
WITH INTEGRATED
ELECTRIC MOTOR

CYLINDERS:
4

GEARBOX:
7-SPEED

TRANSMISSION:
**REAR-WHEEL
DRIVE**

The Mercedes logo sits in the middle of the radiator grille.

A bag inflates from the centre of the steering wheel.

A bag by the driver's knees protects the legs.

SAFE AND SOUND
The car is fitted with a system of seven airbags that inflate automatically in a crash. There are two bags to protect the driver and the front seat passenger from a head-on collision, while bags in the front seats provide further protection. Window bags cover the side windows to protect against an impact into the side of the car.

MAXIMUM POWER: 204 HP AT 3800 RPM

SUSPENSION:	BODY:	BRAKES:	FUEL CONSUMPTION:	CO₂ EMISSION:
FULL AIR SUSPENSION	ALUMINIUM/STEEL	CERAMIC DISCS	3.6 L/100 KM	94 G/KM

CADILLAC ONE

The car flies the US flag and also the flag of the country the president is visiting.

'THE BEAST'

The heavily armoured Cadillac One has been nicknamed 'The Beast' by US security agents. The exact details of its construction are a secret, but it is built to be bullet- and bomb-proof. It is completely airtight to guard against chemical attacks and has its own oxygen supply. The fuel tank is surrounded by foam to stop it from exploding if the car is hit.

The presidential state car, known informally as 'Cadillac One', is a very special car built to carry the US president. It is a limousine with space for seven people. Its design is based on the Cadillac DTS, but this one-off model is heavily adapted. It has the comfort of a luxury car, but is as strong as a tank.

The doors are 20 cm thick and weigh as much as the cabin doors on an aircraft.

| TOP SPEED: | 100 KM/H | FUEL ECONOMY: | 30 L/100 KM |

WELL SUPPLIED

Cadillac One is regularly checked by engineers to ensure that there are no weak spots. But it carries plenty of emergency supplies in case something goes wrong. The boot stores firefighting equipment, a range of weapons, including tear gas canisters and shotguns, and even a supply of blood matching the president's blood type.

The windows are made of several layers of glass and plastic, making them completely bullet-proof.

The tyres are reinforced with super-strong **Kevlar**.

INTERIOR

With its extra-thick doors and windows, Cadillac One is smaller inside than it might appear, but it still has space in the back for the president and four other passengers. It is fitted with a satellite telephone that has a direct line to the Pentagon.

Next to the president's seat is a panic button, which only he can reach to call for help.

GLOSSARY

Aerodynamic
Shaped to minimize a force called air resistance.

Aero splitter
A bar at the front of a car that disrupts airflow to produce downforce.

Carbon fibre
A strong but lightweight modern material.

Chassis
The frame or skeleton of a car to which the car's body and engine are attached.

CO₂ emissions
A measure of the quantity of the gas carbon dioxide that is given off in a car's exhaust fumes. Carbon dioxide is a 'greenhouse gas' that causes global warming.

Cubic centimetre (cc)
A unit of measurement used to describe engine size. There are 1,000 cubic centimetres in a litre.

Cylinder
A chamber in the engine inside which pistons pump up and down to produce power.

Driveshaft
A system of rods that connects the engine to the gearbox, or the gearbox to the wheels.

Exhaust
Waste gases produced by burning fuel in the engine. The exhaust fumes are pushed out of the car through exhaust pipes.

Fascia
A decorative panel on the dashboard of a car.

Fibre-optic
Thin threads of glass or plastic through which a beam of light passes.

Fuel economy
The rate at which a car uses fuel. It is measured in units of litres per 100 kilometres.

Gearbox
A system of cogs that transfers power from the engine to the wheels. Low gears give extra power for acceleration or driving uphill. High gears are used at faster speeds.

Horsepower
A measure of the power produced by a vehicle's engine.

Hybrid
A car powered by both a petrol engine and an electric motor.

Hydraulic
Powered by a system of pipes containing pressurized liquid or gas.

Kevlar
A synthetic material that is five times as strong as steel. Kevlar is used to reinforce tyres and also to make body armour.

Performance

A measure of a car's handling. It includes top speed, acceleration and ease of taking corners.

Powertrain

The path along which power is transferred inside a car. It starts at the engine, then passes through the gearbox and along a driveshaft to end at the wheels.

Satellite navigation

Often abbreviated to 'sat nav', a computer system that uses information beamed from satellites to show drivers where they are and tell them which route to take.

Spoiler

A bar at the back of a car that interrupts the flow of air over the car. This produces downforce, which helps the car to grip the road.

Surround sound

A speaker system that gives listeners the feeling that sounds are coming from all around them.

Suspension

A system of springs and shock absorbers that makes the ride smoother as the wheels pass over bumps in the road.

Transmission

The system of gears that carries the power of the engine to the wheels. The power may be transferred only to the rear wheels, only to the front wheels, or to all four wheels.

Turbocharger

A mechanism that uses the flow of exhaust fumes to produce energy that is used to squash the air inside the engine. This gives the engine more power.

⚙ **www.topgear.com**
The website of the BBC TV series *Top Gear*, which features reviews of the latest cars, interactive games and clips from the show.

⚙ **www.carmagazine.co.uk**
Website of the magazine *Car*, with reviews, videos and photos of a wide range of cars, plus news of upcoming models.

⚙ **www.speedhunters.com**
Features on all kinds of cars, from cutting edge to classic. Speedhunters is run by a group of enthusiasts who post interesting stories from all parts of the world.

⚙ **www.bentleymotors.com**
Website of manufacturer Bentley Motors, with information about their latest models and past models, and a look at some of the best driving routes on the planet.

⚙ **www.jaguar.co.uk**
Website of manufacturer Jaguar Cars, featuring info on their latest models and a glimpse of the future with their concept cars.

⚙ **www.rolls-roycemotorcars.com**
Official website of the luxury car manufacturer Rolls-Royce, with images and technical information, and a history of the company.

INDEX

TOP MARQUES

Titles in the series

WHAT IS A LUXURY CAR?
THE HISTORY OF LUXURY CARS
ROLLS-ROYCE WRAITH
AUDI A8 W12 QUATTRO
BMW 5 GRAN TURISMO
LEXUS LS 600H
PORSCHE PANAMERA
BENTLEY CONTINENTAL GTC
INFINITI Q70
JAGUAR XJR
CADILLAC XTS
MERCEDES-BENZ C300
CADILLAC ONE

9780750285902

WHAT IS A RACING CAR?
THE HISTORY OF RACING CARS
MERCEDES-BENZ F1 W05
DALLARA DW12 INDYCAR
CHEVROLET SS NASCAR RACE CAR
AUDI R18 E-TRON QUATTRO
BMW MINI ALL4 RACING
FORD FIESTA RS WRC
CITROËN C-ELYSÉE WTCC
SPARK-RENAULT SRT 01E
VOLKSWAGEN POLO RX SUPERCAR
TOP FUEL DRAGSTER
LE MANS 24-HOUR RACE

9780750285896

WHAT IS A SUPERCAR?
THE HISTORY OF SUPERCARS
LAMBORGHINI AVENTADOR ROADSTER
MCLAREN P1
ARIEL ATOM V8
KOENIGSEGG AGERA ONE:1
BUGATTI VEYRON
PAGANI HUAYRA
PORSCHE 918 SPYDER
FERRARI LA FERRARI
NISSAN GT-R
CHEVROLET CORVETTE STINGRAY
CONCEPT CARS

9780750285872

WHAT IS AN OFFROADER?
THE HISTORY OF OFFROADERS
PORSCHE CAYENNE TURBO
LAND ROVER RANGE ROVER
NISSAN NAVARA
TOYOTA LAND CRUISER
MERCEDES-BENZ G-CLASS
JEEP WRANGLER RUBICON
BOWLER EXRS
BRABUS B63S
CHEVROLET TRAX
MERCEDES-BENZ UNIMOG
DAKAR RALLY

9780750285889

Get the low-down on some of the coolest,
fastest and most expensive cars in the world.